ASIAPAC B

Stories of Courage

Illustrated by Huang Qingong
Translated by Alan Chong

ASIAPAC • SINGAPORE

Publisher
ASIAPAC BOOKS PTE LTD
996 Bendemeer Road #06-09
Singapore 339944
Tel: (65) 6392 8455
Fax: (65) 6392 6455
Email: asiapacbooks@pacific.net.sg

Come visit us at our Internet home page
www.asiapacbooks.com

First published June 2001 as *Against All Odds*
ISBN 978-981-229-232-2

This revised edition
First published March 2010

ISBN 978-981-229-527-9

Illustrations on pages 72 and 86 are drawn by Tan Meng Hui.

Cover illustration by Huang Qingrong
Cover design by Steve Wan
Body text in 8pt Helvetica
Printed in Singapore by FuIsland Offset Printing (S) Pte Ltd

Publisher's Note

Whilst much emphasis is placed on quick information in today's knowledge-based economy, any "learning nation" must have the wisdom to discern critical attitudes which will help her people withstand the stress of modern living.

In his bestselling book *Principle-Centered Leadership*, Stephen R. Covey contends that the leader of the new millennium is one who creates a culture or a value system centred upon principles. Conceived along this line, the books in the ***Values for Success*** series throw the spotlight on people exalted for possessing a particular virtue. It is our hope that our readers will be inspired by these stories and that they see how practicable the values are, as demonstrated by these people.

We would like to express our heartfelt gratitude to Huang Qingrong for his illustrations, Y N Han for her translation, and the production team for putting in their best efforts to make this publication possible.

VALUES FOR SUCCESS

Stories of Courage

The stories in this book encourage us to cherish big dreams and to never give up. Be inspired by heroes like Ludwig Beethoven, Abraham Lincoln and Helen Keller as they rise above their life challenges.

150x210 mm, 128pp, comics, ISBN 978-981-229-527-9

Stories of Compassion

A little kindness goes a long way. Individuals like Mother Teresa, Florence Nightingale, Albert Schweitzwer and Jane Goodall take many extra miles towards improving the lives of others.

150x210 mm, 136pp, comics, ISBN 978-981-229-528-6

Stories of Intelligence

Offers a glimpse of the childhood escapades and hardships of 13 young people, showing how they adopt a creative approach to handling life's challenges. Read about Isaac Newton, George Washington and more.

150x210 mm, 128pp, comics, ISBN 978-981-229-529-3

Stories of Excellence

The Nobel Prize Laureates in this book have demonstrated their love for Mankind through their back-breaking endeavours. Witness the noble spirit of Alfred Nobel, Albert Einstein, Marie Curie and the like.

150x210 mm, 144pp, comics, ISBN 978-981-229-530-9

Stories of Peace

Selected from Chinese, Indian, Western and other cultures, these stories will surely deepen our understanding of a fact — peace is an everlasting shared goal of all human beings.

150x210mm, 128pp, ISBN 978-981-229-428-9

About the Illustrator

Huang Qingrong 黄庆荣, also known by the name of Ng Keng Yeow, was born in 1975 in Malaysia. He graduated from the One Academy of Communication Design in 1996. On 1997, he worked as an assistant to Taiwanese cartoonist Ai Leidi 艾雷迪. In the same year, he won the second prize in the Fourth Newcomer Comic Award by Sharp Point Publishing. He then came to Singapore to work with Singapore cartoonist Teo Seng Hock 张胜福 in the six-volume *Water Margin* comic series published by Asiapac Books. Other works also published by Asiapac Books include *Stories of Integrity*, *Stories of Kindness*, *Stories of Love* and *Supreme Wisdom*. His other works include short comics on love and science fiction which have been serialised in a Malaysian comic magazine.

Contents

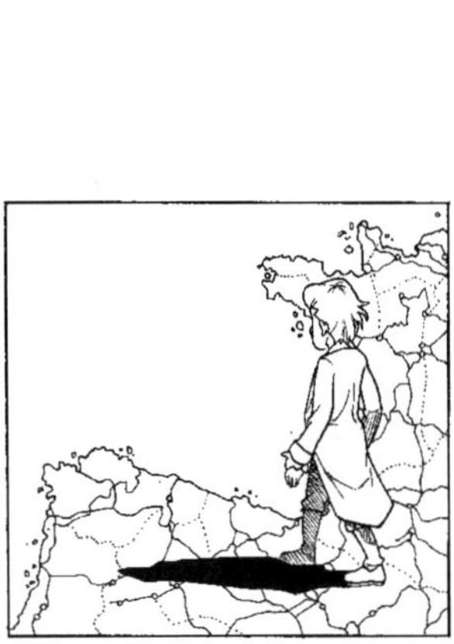

An Unyielding Spirit —
Ludwig van Beethoven (1770 - 1827)

Born in Bonn, Germany, Beethoven is a world-renowned composer. His life was one filled with trials and obstacles. Despite having suffered so much in his life, Beethoven remained optimistic and was determined to extol the joy of life.

Beethoven grew up in a musical family. His paternal grandfather was a well-respected tenor and orchestra conductor with the palace. Under his grandfather's influence, the young Beethoven's love for music was nurtured. Unfortunately, his grandfather passed away when he was three.

Beethoven's father was a mediocre tenor who would flare up easily and had a weakness for alcohol. His mother was a maidservant. She was a loving mother. But she died when Beethoven was 17. Beethoven had two younger brothers.

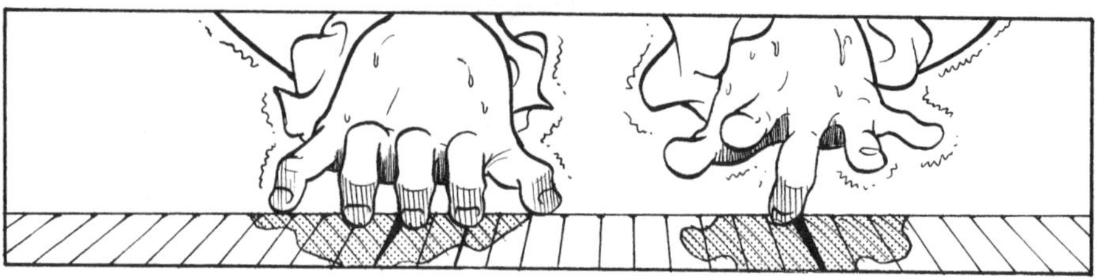

Mozart (1756 – 1791) was a music maestro born 14 years before Beethoven. Born in Austria, he started composing music when he was four years old. At six, he was already performing all over Europe. That earned him the reputation as a child prodigy. However, Mozart had suffered ill health since he was a child. He passed away in his prime when he was 35. Even while he was bedridden, he continued to write music, leaving behind more than 600 pieces of music in his short life.

Vienna, the capital of Austria, is a world-famous music city. Many renowned musicians had lived in Vienna at one time or another. They include the 'Father of Symphony' Handel, music prodigy Mozart, 'Master of Song' Schubert and the 'Saint of Classical Music' Beethoven.

Vienna had no lack of famous music and drama learning institutes, opera houses and concert halls. Even today, music, operas and dramas still play an important part in the lives of the people in Vienna.

At the same time, Beethoven got to know an adorable girl.
Mr Beethoven, she is Miss Giulietta Guicciardi.
Mr Beethoven, I admire your music talent greatly. You must take me under your tutelage.
Sure. That will be my honour.
Beethoven was in love.
However, fate dealt him a heavy blow at the height of his fame and happiness.
One day...

What's wrong with my ears?! Why do I keep hearing mosquitoes buzzing in my ears?!
From then on, Beethoven experienced the buzzing sound in his ears day and night. He was losing his hearing gradually.
Ah… my hearing! Why?!
He kept his hearing problem from everyone and lived as a recluse.
He was soon dealt another blow.
?!
What? You're getting married?!
Count Wenzel Robert has proposed to me.

* A document in which you state what is to be done with your money and property when you die.

Ah, what warm sunshine!
As he walked across a meadow, he enjoyed the wind on his face and the fragrance of flowers tingling his nose…

This is the music of nature!
My hearing may be failing me, but I can still 'hear' the vitality and melody of nature!
Nothing can beat the music of nature. But how many people actually get to hear such heavenly sounds?
I'm going to turn them into music and dispel the misery of life! O Fate, I'm going to grab you by the throat. Never will I bow down to you!

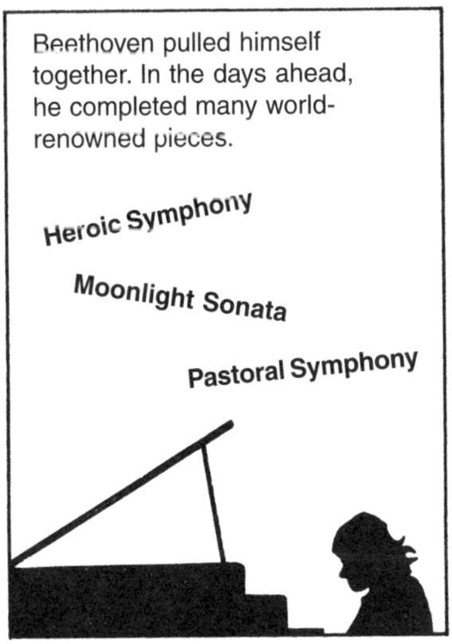
Beethoven pulled himself together. In the days ahead, he completed many world-renowned pieces.
Heroic Symphony
Moonlight Sonata
Pastoral Symphony

The unrestrained force, fire, joy and emotions of life expressed in his music led the way in the Romantic movement in classical music. He also became recognised as a classical composer.

In his twilight years, the totally-deaf Beethoven had to face another heart-wrenching setback.
When he was 53, Beethoven was conducting the *Fidelio* during a rehearsal...
Unable to hear the singing onstage, the orchestra led by him couldn't keep in pace with the singer.
... ...
What happened?
!

Please stop conducting. Will tell you the reason later...
Beethoven was overcome with shame and fury. In a huff, he dashed home.
Is it over for me? Does that mark the end of my music career? No! No! I mustn't bow down to fate!
Beethoven worked harder than he ever did before. In order to 'hear' the music, he used a wooden stick.
One end was placed inside the piano while the other end was held between his teeth. He used the vibration of the stick to help him read the music notes. It was a very tedious process...

After two years, Beethoven gave an inaugural performance of his *Symphony No. 9* at the Karinthian Gate theatre.
Once again, Beethoven led the orchestra.
Under Beethoven's baton, beautiful music was given full rein.
Glad as burning suns that glorious
Through the heavenly spaces sway,
Haste ye brothers, on your way,
Joyous as a knight victorious...
Thunderous applause filled the concert hall. But with his back to the audience, Beethoven was totally unaware of this.
It was not until a female singer took his hand and turned him to the audience…

... that he saw everyone in the hall giving him a standing ovation.

Once again, Beethoven had triumphed over his fate and misery!

Did You Know?

- Much has been said about Beethoven's deafness. It probably resulted from the fact that he suffered from skin tuberculosis, which marred his immune system response, and therefore, his health too. He later died of pneumonia.
- Only five feet five inches tall, he was muscular and thickset, with wide shoulders and a short neck. His face was badly scarred by smallpox.
- Though he was a musical genius, he was poor at spelling and punctuation. He also had problems with multiplication and had awful handwriting.
- *Ode to Joy* is a long poem written by German writer Friedrich Schiller. The poem is about universal joy. Beethoven set it to music and put it right at the end of *Symphony No. 9*.
- Beethoven never married but proposed to many women!
- It is said that his funeral was attended by some 10,000 to 30,000 people! Among the coffin bearers was Franz Schubert, another musical giant.
- You might like to sample some of his works like *Moonlight Sonata*, *Symphony No. 5*, *Violin Concerto*, and *Pastoral Symphony*.

What is Classical Music?

It refers to all musical works with thought-provoking content and a perfect artistic arrangement. It dates from the later half of the 18th century to the 1820s. The music reflected the people's desires and pursuit of life's joys.

Great musicians from that era include Handel, Mozart and Beethoven. These three men had their own styles and had been described thus: Handel is like a joyful stream; Mozart is a lake that is serene and full of ripples at the same time; Beethoven is like a raging ocean!

Find Out More on the Net!

- www.lucare.com/immortal/
- www.kingsbarn.freeserve.co.uk/

The Ugly Duckling —
Hans Christian Andersen (1805 - 1875)

Born in Denmark, Andersen is a world-famous master of children's tales. Coming from a humble background, he encountered many obstacles in the pursuit of his dreams. But his unwavering determination saw him through — he transformed from an ugly duckling into a beautiful swan.

Although Andersen's father was a cobbler, he loved reading and often recited poetry to the young Andersen. With his deft fingers, Andersen's father taught him how to make all kinds of toys and puppets. Andersen's father was not contented with being a cobbler all his life. He once aspired to become a great soldier, but did not make it. He died a sorrowful man when Andersen was 11.

Andersen was born in Odense, which was once the capital of Denmark. It was an ancient place full of mystery that boasted a vibrant arts scene. It ignited Andersen's many dreams and helped spark off his writing of children's books in his later years.

You don't have what it takes to be an actor. You lack the talent and the looks. You don't cut it.
!!
He then visited the manager of the Royal Theatre.
No! No! You've not been trained in acting.
!
He went to see the principal.
!
Ah! The Royal Music College! I've a pretty good voice. I might be able to perform on stage some day!
But that did not discourage Andersen.
Not bad! Not bad! I'll help you to become one of our singers. You've a bright future ahead of you!

But alas, fate had other plans for him...
Winter came. The thinly-clothed Andersen travelled in the chilly wind...
His vocal cords were damaged as a result of the cold...
Cough! Cough!
Looks like you're unable to sing again.
There is nothing I can do for you. You'd better find a vocation back in your hometown.
Go back to my hometown? I'm almost penniless now... But I shan't give up pursuing my dreams...

Andersen knocked on the doors of various theatre groups tirelessly.
When he was finally accepted...
Everybody, come and see! This is our future star — Andersen!
Andersen
Andersen was given minor parts in plays.
He was also made the butt of jokes. But that did not kill his determination.
I must make it one day!

Andersen recited his works, which were written in his free time, at high-society gatherings.
This young man has a flair for writing.
I think so too.
Encouraged, Andersen took his masterpiece to the Royal Theatre.
If they accept my script, it will be played out on the stage. That will be a greater achievement than acting on stage myself.
But the script was rejected.
I'm sorry to tell you that you lack schooling and knowledge about the theatre. Your play will not go down well with our sharp audience.

Everything I try is a failure! I might as well kill myself in this river.
Andersen remembered his father's words.
Child, you must stick to your own ideals and let nothing get in your way.
Where there's a will, there's a way. I mustn't throw in the towel so easily!
Andersen worked hard at learning about the theatre.
He also worked relentlessly on his plays...
Diligence will make up for my lack of training. If I keep on writing, I will make up for my lack of formal schooling.

Once again, he took a new work to the Royal Theatre.
Chancellor Jonas Collin, the theatre manager, was impressed.
Though the play is still not good enough for the stage, you've shown improvement.
Young man, you're very hardworking. If you receive some schooling, I'm sure you will produce outstanding work.
Andersen's keen desire for learning moved Mr Collin, who sought out learning opportunities for Andersen.
Andersen later studied at the Copenhagen University. During his college days, he studied classical literature conscientiously. That enriched his literary knowledge and writing skills.

Then, he wrote a new book.
We don't publish works by novices.
You're an unknown. Who will buy your books?
No one will buy it. We don't do businesses that will make losses.
No one wants to publish it... Fine! I'll think of a way to publish it myself!
The book received unexpected popularity when it was published. Almost everyone in Copenhagen read the book.
A new star in the literary circle was born.

Andersen later produced another work, which was brought to the stage with the assistance of Mr Collin.
Wonder how the audience will take to it.
Silence.
At curtain call...
Clap!
Clap!
Clap!
That was great! Andersen is simply great!
Wonderful! I've made it. I've finally made it...

Andersen loved to travel. He made more than 30 overseas trips during his lifetime. That was quite a feat during his time. He met many famous writers and artists during his travels. The many interesting encounters also sparked off his imagination and inspired his writing creativity.

However...
This Andersen is such a loser. He actually wrote such juvenile stuff. I'd say he's come to the end of the road.
Is it really that bad?
Perhaps I should stop writing children's tales...
But his stories were very popular among children.
!
Uncle Andersen, when are you going to write us more tales? We can't wait to read them!
I pester Mum to read me one of your stories every night before I go to bed.
Thank you, children. Each time I think of my dull childhood, I feel that I should do something for children. Since they like my stories, I should continue writing them. Let me add some joy to their childhood.

Andersen thus plunged himself into writing for children.
Each time he thinks of a new story, he will share it with a few children.
There was once an emperor who loved beautiful clothes...
He recorded the children's responses in a book.
He would do some research and rewrite several times before deciding on the final story.

Though the stories are for children, I believe their parents will read them too.
My children's tales should provide them some food for thought.

Because of his effort and diligence, Andersen's tales are full of imagination and deep moral values.
The Little Match Girl, *The Emperor's New Clothes*, *The Ugly Duckling*, *The Little Mermaid*... These timeless children's tales have won the hearts of children and adults worldwide. Andersen has become the respected master of children's tales.

Did You Know?

- Andersen penned a total of 168 fairy tales, which were translated into more than 100 languages! His books are one of the world's top-selling titles.
- He tended to be over-punctual and had a habit of arriving at railway stations hours too early. He was also fussy and disliked dirt.
- When staying in hotels, he was sure to bring with him a coil of rope in case there was a fire. Upon leaving a room, he would turn back twice to make doubly sure that the candles were out.
- Before his death, he told a composer preparing the music for his funeral to make the beat keep pace with tiny steps for "most of the people who will walk after me will be children". He eventually died of cancer of the liver.
- When he died, a letter from his first lover, Riborg Voight, was found in a pouch around his neck.

Other Writers of Children's Fairy Tales

• Grimm Brothers' Tales

We'd all heard of or read *Snow White and the Seven Dwarfs*, *Cinderella*, *Sleeping Beauty* and *The Frog Prince*. These stories are a part of the Grimm tales written by a pair of German brothers. The elder brother was called Jacob (1785 – 1863) while the younger one was called William (1756 – 1859). They wrote books as a pastime. In 1812, they published the Grimm Tales, which was based on folklore.

• Oscar Wilde's Tales

Oscar Wilde (1854 – 1900), a famous English writer accomplished in poetry, novels and plays, also wrote stories for children. His father was a dentist while his mother was quite a well-known poet. When in university, he started writing. Wilde was sentenced to two years' jail for slander when he was 41. Upon his release, he moved to France where he lived in poverty and died in sorrow. Wilde's popular works include *The Happy Prince, The Star-Child* and *The Selfish Giant*.

Find Out More on the Net!

- www.geocities.com/Wallstreet/2575/hcand.html
- hca.gilead.org.il

A Crusader —
Abraham Lincoln (1809 - 1865)

Lincoln was the 16th President of the United States of America. This farmer-boy won the respect of millions of people. Despite a life fraught with difficulties, he held on to his undying conviction in freedom and peace.

In America, there was a great disparity in the philosophy, economies and politics between the North and the South. The Northerners were more modern in their thinking but relatively poorer. The Southerners were made up of mostly the aristocrats and the wealthy. They were mainly landlords who relied heavily on the labour of black slaves. A group of extremists in the South even secretly formed the Ku Klux Klan to carry out violent acts against the blacks and threats on the whites who showed sympathy towards the blacks.

Look! This black slave is tall and strong. Who will pay a good price for him?
Blackie, get on your knees and crawl one round!
!!
Down! Down! I told you to kneel, blackie!
St… Stop…
!
It is wrong to trade human beings. But I stutter whenever I talk. I'm not eloquent. How am I going to convince people?
Why do I stutter? I will never be able to express myself this way, let alone speak up for the black slaves.

One day, Lincoln heard a sermon by a preacher.
God gives everyone equal opportunities...
!!

The preacher's fluent and expressive language, gesticulations and facial expressions held the audience spellbound.
Everyone in the audience was captivated by his sermon. They laughed and wept as they listened to him...

This is awesome! If only I could speak as well as he does. I'm sure I will be able to convince everyone to stop trading in black slaves then.
The preacher wasn't born with the ability to speak so well. So long as I'm willing to learn, I believe I will overcome my stuttering.
So, whenever the opportunity arose, Lincoln would attend various lectures and speeches. He observed how the speakers talked, moved their arms, etc.
He read prose and tongue twisters aloud.
Four is... four, Ten... is 10, Fourteen is 14...
Sometimes, he would deliberately start a controversial topic and hone his oratorical skills by debating with others.
How can... we... determine... a person's... position... based on... his... skin... colour?!

Once, he was reciting a prose as he walked along.
He did not realise he had walked into a barley field. From then on, he began reading out loud to stalks of barley.
Lincoln went on to become a lawyer. He fought for his clients in court, thus sharpening his oratorical skills.
You incorrigible liar! How dare you fool the court! The laws of nature are impartial. Nature is the best witness!
Every lie will be exposed in the face of nature.

There was no full moon on 18 October. The moon retired at a quarter past 11. So how could you claim that you saw 'an exceptionally bright moon'?
Lincoln spoke most fluently — he was a sharp contrast to his former self.
Lincoln began his crusade to free black slaves. He ran for an office in the Senate.
A slave is a human being. But the law labels him as an object. How can our democratic nation that was founded on ideals like freedom and equality tolerate the system of slavery?

His suggestion met with strong opposition from the Southern slave-owners.
Slaves are our assets! By abolishing the slave system, you are robbing us of our right to property ownership!
Bang!

So long as the problem of slavery isn't resolved, this country will not have peace and justice. I must hold on to my conviction!

With his deep conviction, Lincoln went on to make speeches about the problem of slavery. As a result, he began to gain some fame.

After eight attempts to win the presidential election, Lincoln was finally elected the 16th President of the United States of America in 1860.
Lincoln is the President!
President Lincoln! President Lincoln!
A wave of panic overcame the Southern slave owners.
We don't recognise this administration!
We want independence!
The Southerners formed the Southern Federation.
Civil war between the North and the South broke out.
Boom!

During the early days of the war, the Northern army lacked able generals and so, fought a losing battle.
Factories closed down one after another and farmlands were abandoned.
The masses began to grumble…
Lincoln started the war!
If this war carries on, we won't be able to survive!
End the war, quick!
If the situation persists, what will become of the country? Should I give up my stand?

If the country disintegrates because of me, won't I go down as a villain in history?
No! This war is fighting for the freedom of mankind. I must hold on to my belief. I mustn't give in!
On 1 January 1863, Lincoln created history.
I hereby announce...
As of today, all black slaves shall be free!

In front of the White House
in Washington DC...
We are free!
President Lincoln,
thank you!
Hail President Lincoln!
Hail President Lincoln!
Hail President Lincoln!
!
Everyone will be a free man today. You must improve your lot and let the whole world know that you are people with talent and means!

The Southern army suffered heavy losses in the war in 1863. The Northern army finally saw the light of victory.
Lincoln's popularity rose.
Many lives were lost in this war. The valour of our warriors has given us a legacy that will never die... We must follow up on their achievements. Let this country once again be a free country...
In 1864, Lincoln was re-elected as the president. In 1865, the Southern army surrendered, thus avoiding a split between the North and the South.

Did You Know?

- Lincoln was nicknamed 'Honest Abe', and was a sincere, fair and straightforward man.
- It is believed that he first learnt to write with charcoal on the back of a shovel. His formal education did not last more than a year.
- He was very tall — a staggering six feet and four inches! As he had long limbs, his trousers often ended up looking too short.
- He paid scant attention to his dressing, and often went around in a battered hat and unpolished boots.
- He was shot in the back of his head by actor John Wilkes Booth on 14 April 1865 at Ford's Theatre in Washington DC.
- Booth broke a leg after he leapt from the President's box onto the stage. He managed to get away — but not for long. He was later trapped in a burning barn and was shot dead.
- Linclon himself passed away the morning after the shooting, without regaining consciousness at all. He was the first American president to be assassinated and he supposedly still haunts the White House.
- His wife later went insane.

Uncle Tom's Cabin

Published in 1852, this American novel exposed the slavery system in the US during the early 19th century. The author, Harriet Beecher Stower, was born to a pastor in the northern part of America. She knew about the cruelty of the slave system when she was a child. The main character in her book was a hardworking black slave called Tom. Tom was sold to a slave trader when his owner ran into huge debts. He suffered greatly before he was finally whipped to death. After the book was published, its popularity led to the anti-slavery campaign that resulted in the civil war between the North and the South. When Lincoln first met Stower, he praised her for being 'the little woman who penned a book that started a war'.

Find Out More on the Net!

- Showcase.netins.net/web/creative/lincoln.html
- www.whitehouse.gov/history/presidents/al16/html

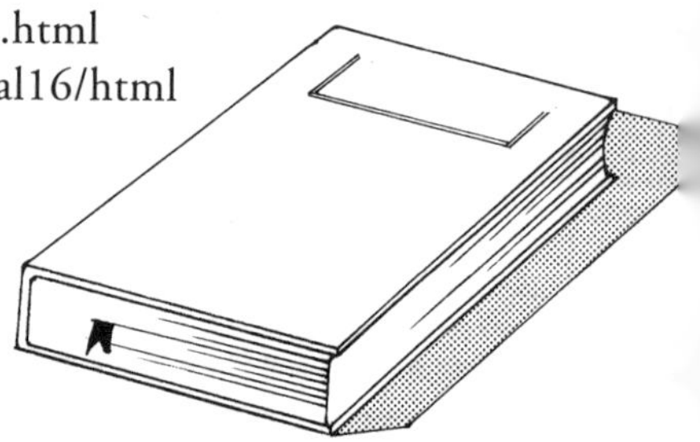

Father of Railroad —
Zhan Tianyou (1861 - 1919)

Zhan Tianyou was an outstanding engineer from China. In his quest to build China's first railroad, he had to endure many difficulties and much mockery. But he did not beat a hasty retreat, and instead, strengthened his resolve. He finally succeeded, boosting the Chinese people's confidence.

Since young, Zhan Tianyou had shown a keen interest in mechanics and science…
Tianyou, what have you done?! You have taken the clock apart!
Mother, I only want to know what keeps the clock ticking away non-stop.
Tianyou, I will take you to a clock shop tomorrow so that you can see how clocks are assembled.
When Zhan Tianyou was 12, he left China to study in the United States of America.

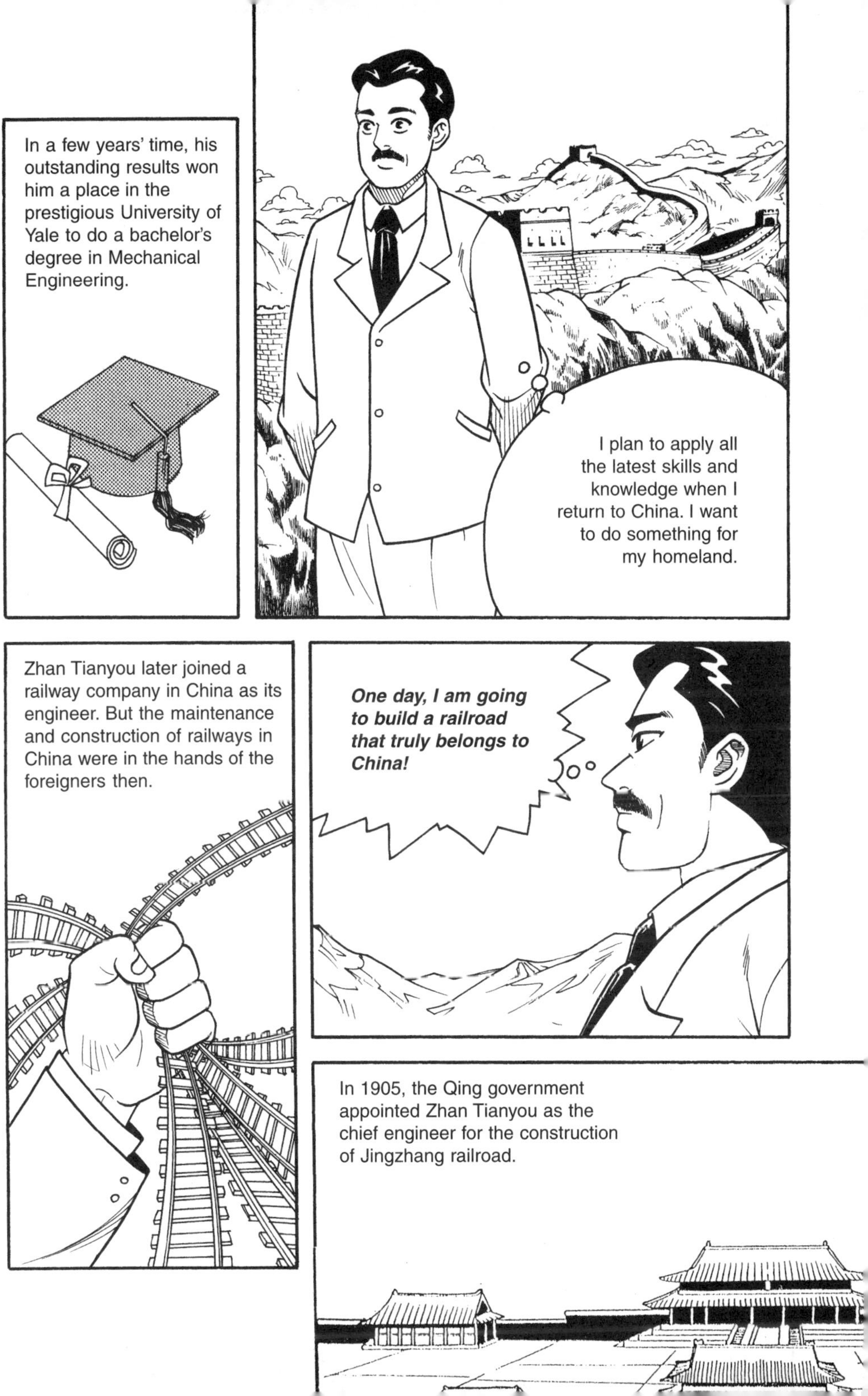
In a few years' time, his outstanding results won him a place in the prestigious University of Yale to do a bachelor's degree in Mechanical Engineering.
I plan to apply all the latest skills and knowledge when I return to China. I want to do something for my homeland.
Zhan Tianyou later joined a railway company in China as its engineer. But the maintenance and construction of railways in China were in the hands of the foreigners then.
One day, I am going to build a railroad that truly belongs to China!
In 1905, the Qing government appointed Zhan Tianyou as the chief engineer for the construction of Jingzhang railroad.

Only Chinese can participate in this project. No foreigners are allowed.
Can these Chinese build a railroad by themselves?
They will come to us for help sooner or later.
I don't care if they doubt our capability or mock at us. I will prove to them that we can do it!
Zhan Tianyou put his heart and soul into the project. He often measured the terrain at the risk of his life in adverse weather.

After several deliberations, he decided on the route.
The route is on a difficult terrain. We also have to build a 3,000-metre tunnel through the mountain. This is an uphill task.
Are you sure you can do it? Such a route is not commonly seen in China or even other parts of the world.
I know. But no matter how difficult the task is, there is a way out.
Zhan Tianyou was deep in thoughts at home one day when his daughter was sewing in one corner.
That's right! I can build the railroad in the same way a pair of scissors moves. I will build it upward along the peak. We'll go round it this way!
In 1905, construction for the Jingzhang railroad began.
Zhan Tianyou was meticulous about the project.
This line is crooked. Redraw it. Remember, everyone involved in this project has to act responsibly at all times. Otherwise, we will fail!

We still need to purchase a lot of materials. But we lack sufficient funds.
Zhan Tianyou had no choice but to approach the merry-making aristocrats for funds.
Duke Sulai, please help. This is for our country…
Ha ha! No problem. Leave it to me. Everybody, bottoms up!
He says 'no problem' each time. But I still don't see the money. No, I mustn't be disheartened. I must persevere.

Besides the lack of funds, Zhan Tianyou also faced many other problems…
Chief, this man tried to damage the railroad while everyone was fast asleep last night.
This railroad will benefit everyone upon its completion. Why would you want to damage it?
Many civilian homes and good farming lands were destroyed to make way for the railroad. How are we going to make a living from now on?
Chief, bad news! Someone is lying on the railroad. He just refuses to get up. He says he won't let the railroad cut through his ancestors' tombs!
!!

Zhan Tianyou plunged into deep thought...
If the construction is going to wreak havoc on the people's lives, it won't be good...
Let's build the railroad at the foot of Mount Dongshan. We'll build an iron bridge. This way, we can avoid tearing down civilian homes.
Thank you! You have our interests at heart!
The construction met with glitches as a result.
Chief, we don't have the Westerners' equipment. It will be difficult to dig a tunnel.

Zhan Tianyou created the 之 (*zhi*) formation of a double carriage moving up a slope in the Jingzhang railroad project. He used two powerful motors to run the train, with one on each end. The front engine will pull while the back engine will push the train forward. This meant that the train would climb up the slope in the *zhi* pattern and when it came to a fork road, the train would change its direction. The head now became the end and vice versa so that the train would continue to scale upwards.

The Jingzhang railway was slated to be completed in six years, but Zhan Tianyou took only four years. Everyone marvelled at his achievement. At the opening ceremony, both locals and foreigners alike came forward to congratulate him.
That was admirable! You have surprised us greatly.
We have to look at the Chinese differently now.
No one had confidence in this project when it first started. That it is operational today is due to the efforts of more than 10,000 workers. I'm but only one of them. Credit isn't mine alone.
Upon Zhan Tianyou's death, the people built a bronze bust of Zhan Tianyou at Mount Bada and a Zhan Tianyou Museum to commemorate the 'Father of Railroad'.

The History of Railroad

In the olden days, men or horses were used to drive a train on the track. Later, the steam engine was used instead.

In 1825, the world's first railroad was seen in England. In order to keep a steam engine going, water, wood or coal had to be added constantly. It was a cumbersome task. Then man learnt to extract petrol and gas from petroleum. The more efficient petrol-run and electric trains in many countries replaced trains running on steam engines.

The Future of Trains

Over the past decade or so, many scientists all over the world have been conducting research on floating trains — air-cushion trains and magnetic trains.

The air-cushion train has no wheels. It ejects pressurised air onto the track, creating an air cushion of about a few millimetres. The train is thus afloat and is pushed forward by a propeller fixed at the back of the train.

In a magnetic train, its wheels are linked through a superconductor with the railway, one that is made of gold and aluminum alloy. It uses the principle of magnetic attraction and repulsion to lift the train between 10 and 20 millimetres off the tracks.

As air-cushion and magnetic trains stay a distance from the track, there is no friction. These trains can thus run at a speed of at least 500 km/h. There will be no vibration, no sound and no pollution. What's more, these trains would not go off-track and run into one another!

Find Out More on the Net!

www.bjmuseumnet.org/museum/zhty/one/htm (Chinese website)

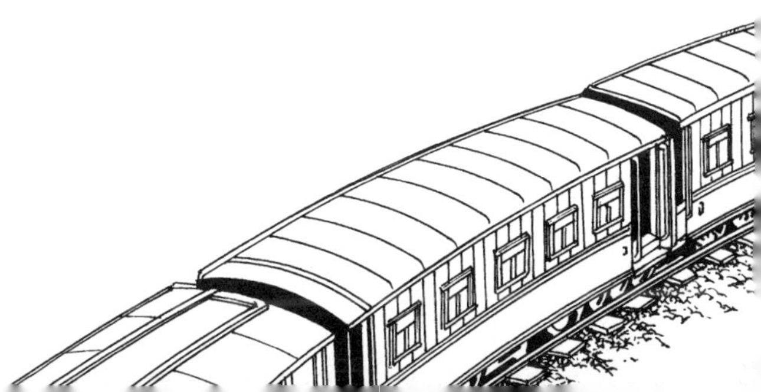

By The Blood-smeared Road — *Mahatma Gandhi (1869 - 1948)*

Gandhi is the spiritual leader behind India's independence. Taking on the powerful British colonial masters, Gandhi started a non-violent movement to lead India towards democracy, peace and independence. Gandhi was jailed several times and hovered on the brink of death in his hunger strikes. Success was finally achieved with his single-mindedness.

Great Britain colonised India in 1877, making it one of the British Empire's many colonies.
He was travelling on the train one day…
Hey! Move your black ass to the third-class carriage!
Having passed the bar examination in 1891, Gandhi left India for South Africa.
!

I bought a first-class ticket. I have the right to sit here!
Indians can only take the third-class carriage. It doesn't matter what ticket you hold!
Gandhi argued with the officer. In the end, he was booted out of the carriage by whites.
Even though the British Empire is powerful, I must rally my fellow countrymen to fight for the right to equality!
Upon his return to India, Gandhi published booklets and gave speeches to raise awareness of how their fellow countrymen were treated overseas.
!!

When he returned to South Africa, Gandhi was recognised on the streets.
?!
That's Gandhi, the Indian blackie who has been badmouthing us!
Give it to him!
?!
One doesn't use tit for tat to disarm one's enemy, but we win them over.
Gandhi struggled in South Africa for more than 20 years. His peaceful movement faced one trial after another. That also served to stretch his patience.

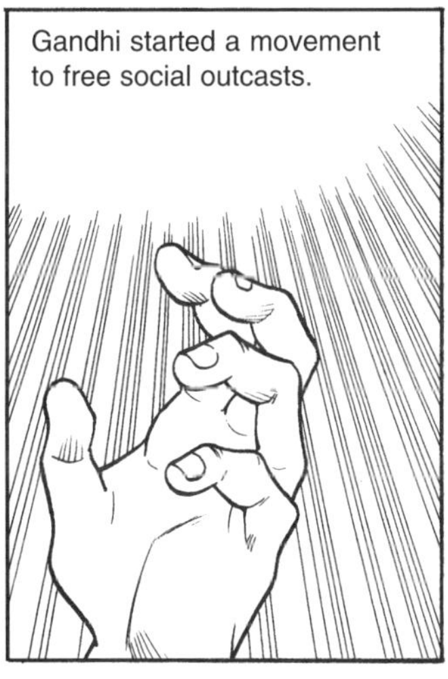

The caste system in India separates society into four classes. Besides these four classes, there is another group deemed the social outcasts (also known as the untouchables). All the things they touch become defiled.

Gandhi organised meeting after meeting to urge everyone to burn Western fabrics and garments.
Everyone shall wear only fabrics made from traditional textile mills!
As the movement for local linen gained momentum, the Indians were swept into the anti-colonial movement.
In 1921, mayhem struck when Prince Edward of Great Britain visited India.
!!
The Indian cotton, *khadi*, is a native product of India. The East India Company bulldozed the cotton fields in India and freighted cotton to England where huge profits were reaped. Huge amounts of English cotton were sold in India, forcing Indian hand-woven cotton factories to close down. Gandhi's cotton campaign aimed to find employment for women from famished farming villages and called for the shutdown of English textile mills.
The riot saw more than 20,000 Indians thrown into jail.

No!
Gandhi hence decided to adopt a peaceful protest. But the situation got out of control.
The mob actually killed a policeman.
Gandhi was willing to be punished for the movement.
I deliberately broke the law. But in my eyes, that's the highest calling for any citizen… I accept the punishment meted out to me by the court.
Gandhi spent his days in jail weaving, reading and reflecting.

The non-cooperation movement crumbled after Gandhi was sent to jail. The once-united Hindus and Muslims were again at loggerheads with each other.
A wave of violence will sweep across the country if the internal unrest is allowed to fester. I must find a way to stop it.
Gandhi went on a hunger strike for 21 days until the two factions made peace.
After his release from prison, Gandhi travelled all over India to unite Indian Hindus and Muslims, abolish the caste system and promote local linen.
Hinduism is India's main religion. During the 8th century, the Moghols built an empire to rule over India. The British later overthrew the Moghols' empire, which left behind lavish mausoleums, Soufie music, palace dance and Islam. Clashes between Hindus and Muslims were frequent.

Our hero Gandhi!
Everywhere he went, he was received warmly by his ardent followers.
Our hero Gandhi!
Our hero Gandhi!
!
No!
Gandhi requested that taxes for land and salt be lowered in 1950. But the colonial government rejected his requests.
Ardent followers of Gandhi hailed him as the Holy Hero. But he did not enjoy being called that. And he did not want to be worshipped like a god. He was an unassuming and approachable person. He called the people close to him 'fathers' and his enemies, his 'brothers'.
He led a group of devotees in a walk that covered 200 miles over 24 days to the western shore of India. This is the famous Salt March.
He scooped up some salt.
Everybody, let's make salt from the seawater!

Gandhi thus broke the table salt monopoly. The colonial government arrested more than 60,000 people.
Gandhi was thrown into jail once again.
I can get more sleep now.
In 1932, the government gave outcasts the right to vote.
What?! This measure will only serve to divide India further!
If the government doesn't change its stand, I will go on a hunger strike until I die.
On the third day of his hunger strike, Gandhi was no longer able to move. He was on the verge of death.

Gandhi went on 17 hunger strikes during his lifetime. He used his own life to spur others to reflect on their own lives, correct wrong ideas and encourage the public that had lost its courage. His hunger strikes succeeded because the people loved him. They did not want him to lose his life because of their mistakes and follies. Gandhi once said: "You only go on a hunger strike for your loved ones. You're not to go on a hunger strike to oppose autocrats."

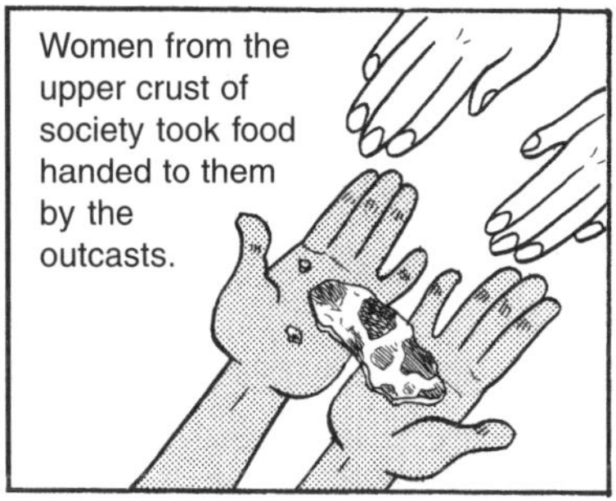

In 1942, Gandhi called for the British to withdraw from India.
Leave India! Leave India!
That landed him in jail again.
I'm going on a hunger strike!
After 21 days of hunger strike, the British government still remained unmoved.
No one… bothers about me… this time…
For the sake of India, I have to end my hunger strike.
We must go independent. What I must do is remove the internal factors that threaten our movement for independence.

In 1946, an inter-religious massacre took place.
Gandhi spread the non-violent approach from village to village.
He turned a deaf ear to the verbal abuse he received and carried on despite stepping on faeces and broken glass as he walked barefooted.
He prayed as he journeyed on.
We all serve one true god. He won't want to see us kill one another.

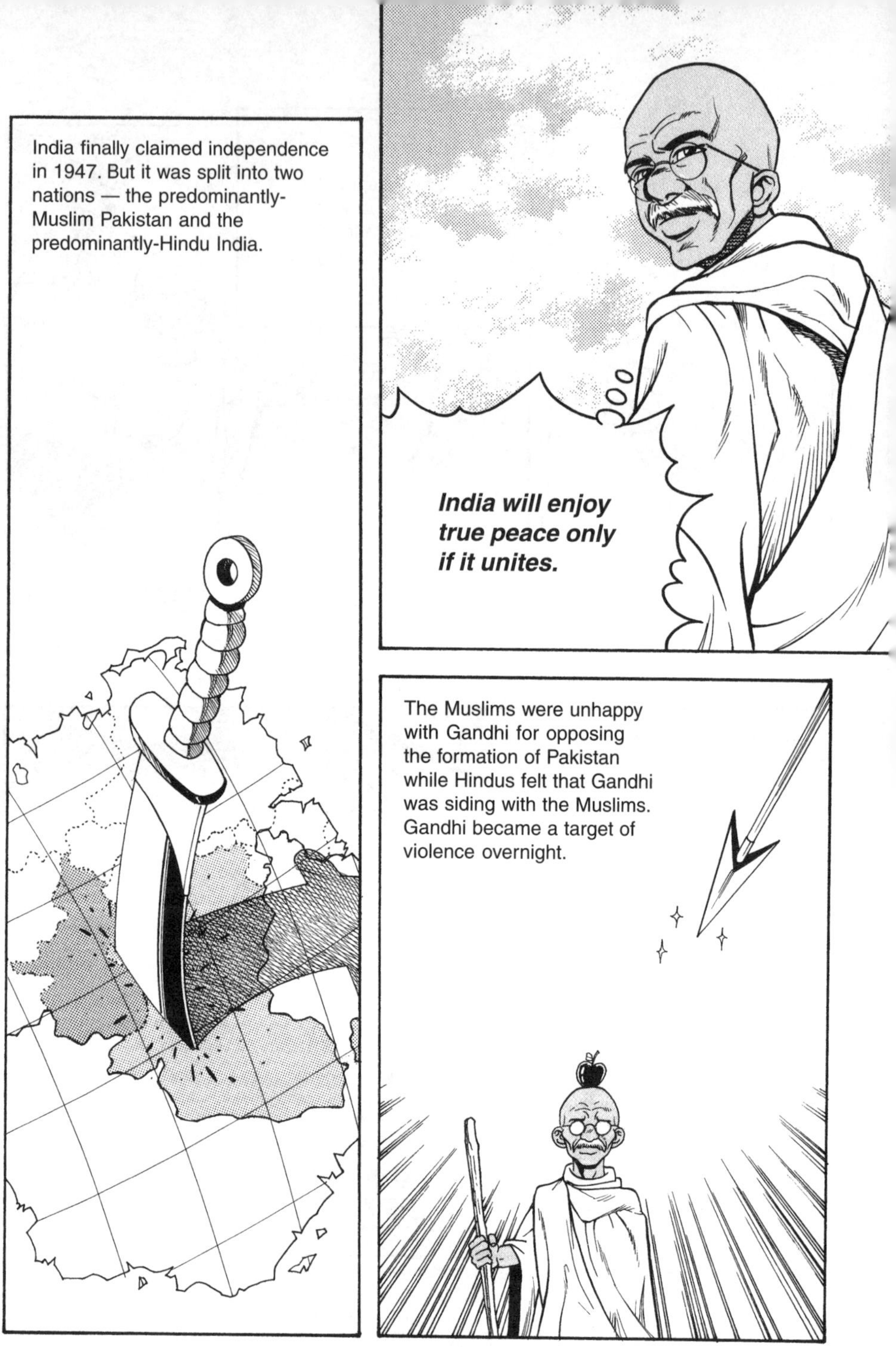
India finally claimed independence in 1947. But it was split into two nations — the predominantly-Muslim Pakistan and the predominantly-Hindu India.
India will enjoy true peace only if it unites.
The Muslims were unhappy with Gandhi for opposing the formation of Pakistan while Hindus felt that Gandhi was siding with the Muslims. Gandhi became a target of violence overnight.

Gandhi carried out a hunger strike in his quest for reconciliation between the Hindu and Muslim factions.

Finally, Hindu leaders promised to stop persecuting the Muslims residing in India. The bloody massacre gradually came to an end…

Gandhi continued to fight for the unity of his countrymen and for religious harmony…
If no one heeds your call, walk on…
If no one dares to speak out of fear, make a loud declaration…
If everyone has left, walk on…
Treading on a thorny path along the blood-smeared way, walk on…

The Great Soul

Mahatma Gandhi was born Mohandas Karamchand Gandhi. He is commonly known as Mahatma Gandhi, where Mahatma means 'Great Soul'.

Gandhi's Pearls of Wisdom

You might find these quotes rather difficult but discuss them with your parents or teachers and you will benefit from Gandhi's wisdom.

Friendship that insists upon agreement on all matters is not worth the name. Friendship, to be real, must ever sustain the weight of honest differences, however sharp they be.

An ounce of practice is worth more than tons of preaching.

Courage has never been known to be a matter of muscle; it is a matter of the heart. The toughest muscle has been known to tremble before an imaginary fear. It is the heart that sets the muscle trembling.

I look only to the good qualities of men. Not being faultless myself, I won't presume to probe into the faults of others.

The real ornament of woman is her character, her purity.

Non-violence is the greatest force at the disposal of mankind. It is mightier than the mightiest weapon of destruction devised by the ingenuity of man.

Glory lies in the attempt to reach one's goal and not in reaching it.

Find Out More on the Net!

- www.cbu.edu/Gandhi/html/chron2/html
- www.mkgandhi.org
- www.kamat.com/mmgandhi/mmgandhi.htm

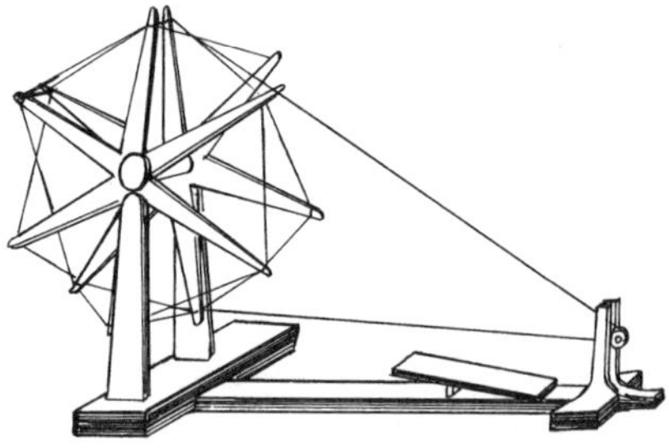

Finding Light in Darkness — *Helen Keller (1880 - 1968)*

A famous American social activist, Keller overcame her physical handicap with extraordinary and steely determination. Not only did she successfully complete her university education, she became a linguist in five foreign languages and wrote 14 classics, creating a miracle in the history of mankind.

Keller was born a healthy and active girl. However, a high fever at the age of one caused her to lose her sight and hearing.
Since then, she plunged into a world of darkness and deafening silence.
She thus lost her ability to speak and express her emotions.
Helen... what are you trying to say?
Ya... ya...
Ah, she's always struggling to express herself, but we cannot understand her...

Keller kept struggling to 'talk' though no one could understand her...
Ya ya ya!
Crash!
Bang!
Yi ya!
Ya... ya...
Helen, don't do that! Stop it!
My poor child. If this goes on, what shall we do?

Keller's parents were very upset at the sight of their beloved daughter's plight.
But Keller's pain and suffering was unspeakable. No matter how hard she tried, she could not set herself free from her dark world.
I want to get out! I do not want to stay in this silent and lifeless world!
When Keller turned seven, her parents employed a governess for her — Anne Sullivan.
Anne Sullivan lost her eyesight suddenly when she was 14. She then received education at a school for the blind. She regained her sight when she underwent an operation a year later. This experience spurred her to study hard and become an outstanding teacher.
Sullivan first began by correcting some of Keller's bad habits.
During mealtimes, use your fork and not your hand. Come, try it.
Whenever Keller threw tantrums, Sullivan would not intervene until the former had calmed down.
Ya ya ya!

Sullivan gave Keller a doll, and slowly spelt the word 'doll' on Keller's palm.
D-o-l-l.
Keller was fascinated, and did the same on Sullivan's palm.
D-o-l-l.
That was the beginning of Keller's learning process.

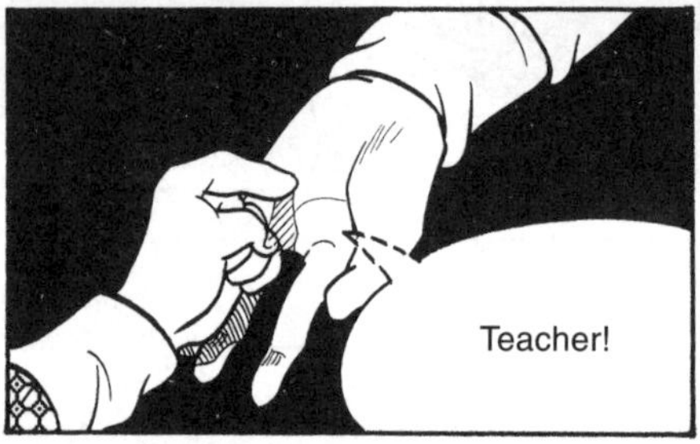

Braille cards and books are special books for the visually handicapped. Dots that jut out form the words in a Braille book. When the blind reads, he or she touches the dots line by line to make out the word based on the number of dots and their arrangement.

Later, Keller attended a school for the blind, and learnt to use sign language to communicate and play games with her newfound friends.
An avid learner, Keller often immersed herself in books at the school library to widen her general knowledge.
Using her finger, she studied numerous subjects like Mathematics, Geography, History and Biology and also mastered several languages.
Keller still had one unfulfilled wish.
How wonderful it would be if I could only speak!
Though I can neither see this beautiful world nor hear the different melodious sounds, I still hope to be able to use words to express my love for this world.

Keller relayed her wish to Sullivan.
This is going to be a very difficult task. But I believe that you can achieve it, Helen.
Sullivan brought Keller to see a lady who specialised in training deaf-mute students to speak.
Taking Keller by her hand, the lady placed it on her own jaw and throat, and began to produce sounds. It was an extremely slow and difficult learning process.
‘i’
She wanted Keller to imitate her by using her hand to adjust her teeth and tongue properly in order to produce the correct sounds.

Keller tried very hard to produce the right sounds. She would often perspire in her attempts to produce the right sounds for even a simple-sounding letter.
... 'i' ...
At home, Keller asked Sullivan to practise with her.
M... n...
No, Helen. It's m... n...
m... m...
After days and nights of endless practice, Keller could finally speak.
Wea... ther... very... hot...
Having overcome her inability to speak, Keller continued to learn to speak French, German, Latin and other foreign languages.
Helen is indeed capable.

Madam, I must improve further! My goal is to study at Harvard University.
Helen, I am behind you!
To gain admission into university, Keller studied at a girls' college located near Harvard University.
Sullivan would sit beside Keller in classes, penning down the lecture notes on Keller's palm.

After school, Keller would often stay up past midnight to type out whatever she could remember of her lessons on her Braille typewriter.
Ta... ta... ta...

In 1900, when Keller was 20 years old, she was admitted to Harvard University through the university entrance examination.
I've made it! Madam, I've finally made it!

In 1904, Keller's impressive results led her to become the world's first blind-and-deaf university graduate.

Everyone applauded her accomplishment.
What a noteworthy achievement!
She is a fabulous role model!
I owe what I achieve today largely to Miss Sullivan. I plan to follow in her footsteps by giving myself to the education of the blind and deaf-mute.
Keller started giving speeches and donating to the cause of those who were blind and deaf-mute.
Having eyes that cannot see, ears that cannot hear, living in a colourless and unexciting world, being unable to hear the sounds of this world, is a very painful thing.
We have so many such unfortunate people in our society today. I hope that everyone can contribute towards the education of the deaf-mute and blind, helping them to walk out of their darkness and silence...

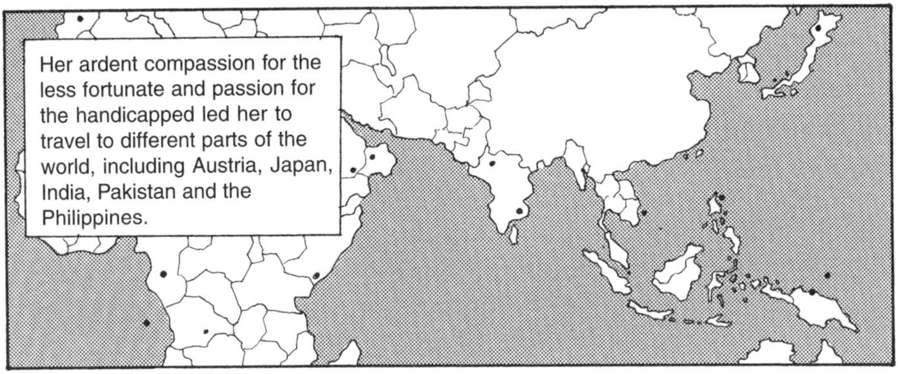
Her ardent compassion for the less fortunate and passion for the handicapped led her to travel to different parts of the world, including Austria, Japan, India, Pakistan and the Philippines.

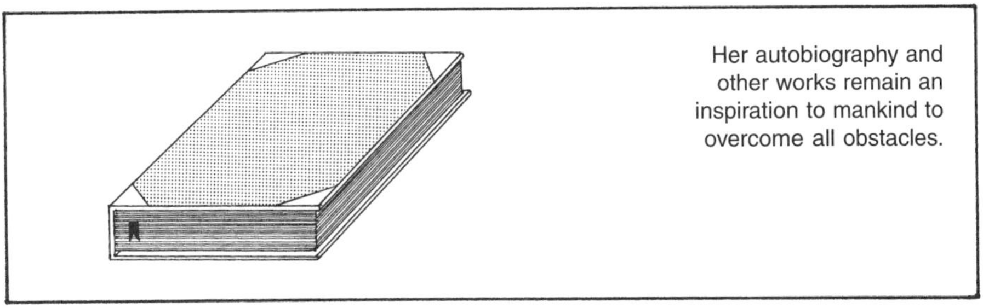
Her autobiography and other works remain an inspiration to mankind to overcome all obstacles.

Life will be very meaningful if everyone can briefly experience what it is like to be blind and deaf during his or her youth. The darkness will cause him to treasure life even more, and the loneliness will cause him to cherish the sights and sounds around him…

Sign Language

Sign language is an international system of hand signals that replaces verbal communication. It uses fingers to represent the alphabet and hand signals. The hearing-impaired often use sign language to communicate with others. Like all other languages, it has different versions because of differences in customs, living habits, history and culture in various countries.

Sign language was first used in convents and monasteries, which observed strict rules where silence had to be maintained. Hence, the monks and nuns used sign language to communicate with one another.

During those days, deaf-mute children were sent to convents and monasteries at a young age as their families wanted to keep their condition hush-hush. These children picked up sign language to 'talk' to others. In time to come, sign language became common and spread to other deaf-mute learning institutes.

Let's look at some interesting hand signals. The ones used here are from the American Sign Language (ASL).

Thank you

Hello

Sorry

I love you

Good luck

Find Out More on the Net!

- www.mib.org.uk/wesupply/fctsheet/keller.htm
- helen-keller.freeservers.com

A Bumpy Ride to Stardom — *Charlie Chaplin (1889 - 1977)*

Born in England, this world-renowned comedian and artiste had a difficult childhood. Though he was born with the innate talent to be a comedian, the glorious career he carved out was achieved only after many failures.

A singer past her prime was singing on stage when she suddenly lost her voice. The audience booed and jeered at her.
Boo!
Get lost!
How shall I handle this sticky situation?
Mother, are you all right?
Got it. This child often watches you sing. Let him perform in your place.

* A song made popular by comedian Gus Elen about the behaviour of a man named Jack Jones who had inherited some money.

This five-year-old boy who came to his mother's rescue was none other than Charlie Chaplin, who later brought much laughter to audiences worldwide.
Chaplin's parents divorced when he was young. His mother supported herself and her young son on the miserable pay she earned as a singer. Life was difficult.
His mother later went insane. Following that, Chaplin put up at an apprentice centre for the poor and an orphanage. He even became a street urchin at one point.

To make ends meet, he worked as a delivery boy for a grocer, sold flowers, worked as a servant, sold newspapers, and sold discarded items… But he had a dream.
I shall become an actor one day.
When he was 12, he knocked on the door of a casting agency for actors.
As the days passed by...
Sir, do you need someone to play the role of a child?
We are going to produce *Jim — A Romance of Cockayne*. You will play the part of a newspaper delivery boy.

Great! My dream is going to be realised. If I succeed, I will break free from poverty!
Chaplin put his heart into his role and brought life to his character. Though the play was not a success, Chaplin's acting received good reviews.
But Chaplin's acting career was not smooth-sailing. When he was 17, he went to audition for a part in a comedy that he had written.

He was full of expectations. He imagined himself to be famous after the performance and that money would roll in. He'd buy a mansion and drive a big car…
Comedy master with impeccable comic timing that will leave you in stitches — Charlie Chaplin!
He finally got to perform his own play…
!
Ah?!
Get off the stage!
To think he had the cheek to do such an unoriginal story!
Get off the stage!
Chaplin was brought down to earth. He reflected on his failure.
It was a flop. Why? Perhaps I lack the experience and the theme wasn't original enough. I'm not suited to be a stage actor… But I still believe I'll make a good comedian. I must keep on trying!

He wrote another comedy, which was bought by a vaudeville investor.
Mr Chaplin, here's three pounds. You will direct it.
Chaplin began preparations with great excitement. He put together a cast.
!
But on the third day of rehearsal, his sponsor sent him a note.
What?!
He wants out! How am I going to tell the cast? Why am I always so unlucky?

With my talent and hard work, I believe I will make my mark! The day will come when my talent will be discovered!
The day finally came. He was invited to act in the play *The Football Match*.
I'm going to create some actions for this role…
In order to play his part well, Chaplin went to catch performances of the same play.
The actor isn't natural. This role needs to have more comic flavour. There should be more spontaneity.

His chance to perform finally came. Chaplin was very nervous.
How will the audience respond?
Don't be nervous. I have made ample preparations. Just put my heart into it.
Ah ha!
Ha ha ha!
His performance was a great success. Everyone congratulated him.
That was excellent!
No one has ever played that role this well!

Chaplin travelled with the troupe to perform in America.
I hear America is an exciting and adventurous place. I'm sure I can carve out a career here.
Though his performance was well received, Chaplin did not get any opportunity to develop his career there.
America, I will be back.
Chaplin left for America again in 1912. His acting talent was discovered by Mack Sennett of Keystone Film Company. He was paid handsomely to act in comedies.
I'm going to appear in movies! That's a brand new arena. I will be able to further my comedy career… But if I fail, poverty will greet me once again…
No! This is a golden opportunity. I can't back out just because I'm afraid.

Chaplin finally made up his mind to give it a go…
As film companies had no scripts then, many of the comic moments were added on the spur of the moment. Chaplin acted his heart out.
He even gave the director suggestions.
Sir, if we do it that way, we will have the audience in stitches.
But he was greatly disappointed when he saw the final version.
Whatever happened?!

Why did they edit my funny parts?
Why did they do this...?
It turned out that the director was jealous of his talent.
I'm the director! I have the final say. I'll edit whatever I want!
Chaplin could only bide his time.
Then Sennett sent for Chaplin.
!
You'll be playing a joker. You're free to do whatever you want.

Boss, what do you think of this?
Look, this chap is multi-faceted. He is a tramp, a gentleman, a poet and a dreamer. He is lonely and is always dreaming of a romantic life that involves risky adventures.
Ha ha ha!
La la la...
Huh?
Ha ha ha!

Whenever it was Chaplin's scene, the crew would all gather to watch him in action. Everyone was tickled by his hilarious gestures.
Chaplin successfully created a figure that no one else could imitate. He exposed and made fun of some social conditions through the roles he played. Movie audiences worldwide were thus introduced to Charlie Chaplin, and he won their thunderous applause.
Chaplin starred in 81 movies during his acting career. Most of them were written and directed by the actor himself. He even added in sound effects, conducted the orchestra and choreographed the dance in some of them. He was a man of many talents.

The Magic of Movies

Movies are created based on our ability to retain what we see. When our eyes see light, we retain it for between 0.05 and 0.1 second after it is gone. This is known as sight retention. By running a series of images in quick sequence, a continuous movement is created. We view them as movies.

The History of Movies

Year 1888 – American inventor Edison discovered the movie projector where moving images can be captured through a small hole. In one minute, 40 images are displayed.

Year 1895 – French brothers Lumiere invented the first motion picture projector using light where images were projected onto a screen. It is said that some viewers found a train moving towards them so real that they ran out of the cinema in terror.

Year 1927 – Movies with sound effects were born. Early movies were silent ones with only moving images. But a narrator would explain the movie content to the audience and sound effects like gunshots were also added. Later, a violinist or a band provided music. Chaplin was the most famous actor during the silent movies era.

Year 1950 – Upon the creation of chemically-coloured film, full-colour movies gradually replaced black-and-white ones.

Other Types of Movies

Wide-screen movies: Three cameras placed in front, to the left and to the right, project images onto a screen to create a 2-D effect.

3-D movies: 3-D movies make use of two cameras with colour filters in the shooting process. Two projectors are used during the movie screening. The audience has to put on coloured shades (one side is green while the other side is red). By looking through the two shades, you get a 3-D visual effect.

Smell movies: Films now also come with smells. During the screening of a movie, a smell emitter on every seat will release various smells.

Find Out More on the Net!

- www.geocities.com/Hollywood/Screen/7157

Founder of a Cartoon Empire —
Walter Elias Disney (1901 - 1966)

Born in America, he created the huge cartoon empire that brings endless laughter and joy to children and even adults the world over. His road to entrepreneurship did not come easy — failures, poverty, starvation and betrayal, among others, marked it. But the optimistic man overcame them all...

Disney was born on a farm where he grew up among animals.
Poker, come here!
!!
Be good, stay still. I'm going to draw you.
He loved drawing since he was young. When he grew up, he found employment as an apprentice with an advertising firm.

Disney got to know Ubbe 'Ub' Iwerks, a highly-talented illustrator.
I'm Disney. Nice meeting you.
I'm Iwerks.
It wasn't long before…
!!
The company isn't doing well. We can no longer hire you.
What shall we do now?
It's not easy to find a job. But we can create jobs for ourselves. Let's form an advertising firm. We won't starve to death.
You're on!

Disney actively sought business opportunities after the company Iwerks & Disney was formed.
POST
Sir, your magazine has great potential. But it's still not making money. That's because the look of your magazine is too boring. If you add some illustrations, it will boost sales.
Unfortunately, business was poor and the company folded.
The two men found employment as cartoonists with an animated film company. That was when Disney discovered the charm of animated films.
Animated films are interesting! And it has great potential for growth. This is something worth looking into.

Disney never stopped upgrading himself in this area. He read, went to the movies, shot his own cartoons, etc.
He left the company and used all his savings to set up Laugh-o-Grams.
Iwerks, I've made ample preparations this time. We won't fail!
With his friend's assistance, he completed Puss in Boots, Little Red Riding Hood and other animated films.
Pal, the cartoons are popular! We have made it! Ha ha!
Don't be too happy just yet. Due to our poor handling of accounts, we're now in debt.
!!

Plunged into dire straits, Disney could not even afford decent meals.
Sir, can you pay me in advance?
I've done that many times. We're running a business here.
At least I still have a can of beef to keep me going...
Ring...
Hello, I'd like to commission you to do an animated feature on toothpaste. Can you come over and discuss it?
Er... I can't go over now... My only pair of shoes is torn and has been sent to the cobbler's. They're ready for collection. But as I have no money to pay the cobbler...

The company went bust eventually. Disney had no choice but to declare himself bankrupt.
I only have $50 left. What shall I do? Let's try my luck in Hollywood.
Get lost! There's no job for you here!
After a few failed attempts to get a job...
I still want to be involved in animated films. I don't believe I can't make it.
Disney got his elder brother Roy to invest to start the Disney Brothers' Studio.

Disney worked with a film producer to produce *Alice's Wonderland*. It was a feature that combined both real actors and animated characters. It was very well received when it was released.
Disney later created Oswald the Lucky Rabbit as the lead in an animated feature.
But the film producer Charles Mintz rejected it at its first instalment.
Too many repetitive actions, the story doesn't flow and Oswald is too fat.
Disney redid it and handed in the second instalment. Still, the other party was not satisfied.
!
No!!

Instead of being discouraged, Disney was motivated.
Fine! I'll seek perfection in my future animated features. No slipshod work for me.
The third instalment was finally accepted and the audience loved it.
Just as Disney was having his first taste of major success, a conspiracy was in the works... When Disney was discussing the extension of the contract with the film producer...
What?! You'll only pay me $1800 for each instalment?
It can't even cover production costs! You can't be serious!
If you don't take it, we needn't extend the contract. But the rights to Oswald belong to us. You can no longer draw that rabbit.

In fact, you won't be able to do any more animated features. I have already hired all your illustrators with the offer of a higher pay.
This is the new contract. If you join our company and allow us to have the copyright to the creations, we will offer you 50 percent of the movie profits. What say you?
How can I work for someone who has cheated me? I'd rather start from scratch!
Disney was greatly angered and saddened by the betrayal of his staff and the film producer.
I give up the copyright to Oswald! I don't need him anymore!

But he did not give up
drawing animated features.
I must
create a
new cartoon
icon! I can
do it!
!
Mouse? Let's
draw a mouse!
He observed the movements
of mice carefully…
He drew and redrew
images of a mouse…

What shall I call it? It has to be an easy-to-remember name. Let's call it Mickey! It'll be Mickey Mouse!
Film producers' response to the first instalment of Mickey Mouse was cool.
No one knows Mickey.
Disney did not stop there.
Mickey Mouse must become a household name!
Film producers were still not Interested in the second instalment.
Who would want to watch a mouse?
!

At that time, Hollywood released its first sound movie *The Jazz Singer*.
Disney was inspired…
If I can give Mickey a voice, that will attract people.
In order to pay for dubbing fees, Disney sold his beloved car.
Goodbye!!
The dubbing did not go well. The first recording was a failure.
Blah blah blah...
Let's try again. The sound must be realistic and in sync with the movements!

Though the main characters in Disney cartoons were born in Disney's mind, the realisation of his concepts was left to his illustrators. Disney would first conceptualise a cartoon character's appearance, temperament and traits. He then described his ideas to his team of illustrators, who were responsible for drawing them.

A man who relentlessly broke new ground, Disney decided to move in a new direction when he was 50.
I want to build a dream-like theme park where every child and adult can live out his or her childhood dreams.

Disneyland was officially opened in 1955. This fantasy park attracted visitors from all over the world. This was where they realised their dreams and found joy.

Did You Know?

- Disney liked to be called 'Uncle Walt'.
- During World War I, he lied about his age and served in France as a Red Cross ambulance driver. His ambulance was covered, not with camouflage graphics, but with cartoons.
- He was a heavy drinker and smoked up to 70 specially-rolled black cigarettes a day. As a result, he had a smoker's cough that would not go away.
- He played polo and poker and rode well. In fact, he was a cowboy extra with Warner Brothers.
- He was crazy about trains and had a half-sized steam railway in his garden.
- He was a stickler for cleanliness and washed his hands about 30 times an hour.
- Disney himself did the voice of Mickey Mouse.
- Mickey Mouse made his first appearance on 18 November 1928 and was originally named Mortimer after a real mouse Disney kept as a pet. However, Disney's wife objected so he changed the name to Mickey.

Using Computer Graphics in Cartoons

A 20-minute animated feature requires at least 28,800 drawings. An animated movie will take about four years to complete. That's a massive project! Luckily, the computer illustration system has made this mammoth task much simpler. Production time has been cut to one or two years. The illustrator only needs to draw the first and final movements, and the computer will fill in the movements in between. The illustrator may even do the colouring, correct the characters' movements, change scenes and rearrange the sequences — all on computer!

Find Out More on the Net!

- www.intergraffix.com/walt/xindex.htm
- www.justdisney.com

TOP total skills programme

TOP HEALTH TIPS
Find out how the Top friends keep fit, fight stress and keep the flu at bay. You will be surprised how feelings are a big part in health and vitality!
Ilustrated by **Jack Cheong**,
150x210 mm, 128 pp, ***comics***,
ISBN 978-981-229-521-7

NEW

TOP ECO TIPS
Join the Top Survival friends to save the Earth in this book featuring 18 environment-related stories. Learn 60 tips to protect Mother Nature. Learn to reduce, reuse and recycle, and be an EcoPal!
Ilustrated by **Jack Cheong**,
150x210 mm, 128 pp, ***comics***,
ISBN 978-981-229-514-9

TOP SURVIVAL TIPS
Contains 30 cases to help you cope with crisis situations. Learn how to be alert at all times and save yourself and others from gas leakage, choking, robbery, bee stings, snake bites, earthquakes, etc.
Ilustrated by **Jack Cheong**,
150x210 mm, 128 pp, ***comics***,
ISBN 978-981-229-481-4

TOP CRIME MYSTERIES
TOP CRIME BUSTERS
Learn how the police get to the bottom of mysteries and bring criminals to justice, using the behaviour of insects, the traits of mussels, and even the time flowers bloom.
Ilustrated by **Jack Cheong**,
150x210 mm, 128 pp, ***comics***,
ISBN 978-981-229-460-9 / ISBN 978-981-229-365-7

勇敢的故事

绘画：黄庆荣

翻译：韩 玉

亚太图书有限公司出版